COACH SHANE'S ENGLISH EXPRESSION SERIES

250

AMERICAN

IDIOMS AND PHRASES

(451 to 700) English Idiomatic Expressions

With Practical Examples & Conversations

Written by

Muhammad Nabeel

Author   : Muhammad Nabeel

Edition   : 1st

Date   : August 2016

Author page: www.amazon.com/author/muhammadnabeel

PREFACE

American idioms and phrases book (From English Expression No. 451-700) is in your hand. In last book, you have learnt 450 common English idiomatic expressions. In this book you will learn 250 more fresh American idioms and phrases with practice examples and conversations. This book is for intermediate, advanced level students and foreign speakers.

I picked up these common English expressions from sitcoms, movies, news, etc. Having learned these sayings, idioms and phrasal verbs, you would be able to understand movies, sitcoms, and news. Also you would be able to communicate in all around world. Your listening comprehension would be much better. If you want enrich your vocabulary and increase your word list, it would prove an excellent book.

If you have question, suggestions and opinion, please let me know. I would improve and fixes in upcoming edition.

Signature

Muhammad Nabeel

Muhammadnabeel400@gmail.com

NO.451 - to do my darndest (darnedest)

Meaning: to do my best

Dialogue:

Person A:	How'd Timmy do yesterday?
Person B:	He struck out the one time he was at bat.
Person A:	Aw. That's too bad.
Person B:	I know. He did his darndest, though!

✳✳✳✳✳

NO.452 - What is he to you

Meaning: what is your opinion about him (2) what is your relationship with him

Exp: what is English to you means 'what is your opinion about English.'

Mostly this expression use to describe relationship. What is she to you? Is she your sister or girlfriend? What's the relationship?

Dialogue:

I really hate John.
He's not that bad.
What? What is he to you?
Well, actually he's my sister's boyfriend.

✳✳✳✳✳

NO.453 - I got a beef with you

Meaning: have a complaint

Exp: So if you got a beef with someone, you might wanna fight, you need to argue or talk about something, someone made you mad.

Dialogue:

Hey! I've got a beef with you.
What? What did I do?
You used my cell phone without asking.
Oh, hey, man! Sorry about that. It was an emergency~

✳✳✳✳✳

NO.454 - to tank

Meaning: to run out of, to become empty, to be depleted

Exp: We use this expression, when we talk about our energy. My energy has tanked and now I have no more energy. My faith has tanked, I no longer believe. Something happened and because of something, my faith/belief has zero. My faith has tanked. So faith, belief, motivation, this type of feelings, you can use this expression.

Dialogue:

Hey! How's your English studying going?
Ugh~ My motivation has tanked.
Why? Keep going!
But sometimes it's so hard. I don't think I'm progressing

✳✳✳✳✳

NO.455 - to scoff at -

Meaning: to show you don't like it, you think its stupid/ridicules

Exp: if we don't believe something and if we think that is stupid and not important, we just show that you think it's stupid and you don't believe it and it's not important to you. Then other person could say, 'Don't scoff at me.'

Dialogue:

What do you think of my new suit?
Tsk!

Don't scoff at this! It cost $500!
What? It looks like it's from the dollar store

NO.456 - Great shot!

Exp: When you take a wonderful picture from your smart phone, then you can say 'great shot'

Dialogue:

Check out this picture.
Wow! Who took it?
I did.
Really? Great shot!

NO.457 - leftovers

Exp: food that you had the dinner/lunch but you didn't finish all of the food, and you can throw away the food or you can keep the food and put into the refrigerator and later you can eat them. That's food is the leftovers.

Dialogue:

You want me to throw this out?
No. Put it in the fridge.
Who's gonna eat leftovers?
I will!

NO.458 - midnight snack

Exp: If you are sleeping at night and at midnight, you awake suddenly and you feel hungry, then you go to the kitchen and start eating something. That's the midnight snack.

Dialogue:

What are you doing?
Hiding the leftover steak.
Why?
I want it for my midnight snack tonight. Don't tell dad.

✳✳✳✳✳

NO.459 - hodgepodge

Meaning: a confusing mixture of this & that

Exp: Coach Shane's English expression book is hodgepodge because it has useful idioms, phrases, nouns and lots of other things. It has many things; there is no one related thing. Sometimes this expression may have negative meaning and sometime positive.

Dialogue:

Mm! Something smells good.
It's just a hodgepodge of leftovers.
Is it ready? I'm starving.
In about 30 minutes.

✳✳✳✳✳

NO.460 - to leg it

Meaning: to walk

Exp: when I went to the school, I usually had to leg it. I walked and I never used the bicycle

Dialogue:

How are you getting to the game?
I'll leg it.
It's 3 miles!
So? The weather's perfect for a nice walk

*****

NO.461 – gibberish

Meaning: nonsense

Exp: You are reading something but you don't understand, that is gibberish. Somebody is talking to you but you don't understand, it is gibberish.

Dialogue:

So, how is Shane's DDM class?
Well, the news stories are pretty easy, but that situation comedy~ Ugh! A bunch of gibberish!
Well, situation comedies give you real, daily English. Study hard.
I know~ I won't give up!

*****

NO.462 - to be tied up with something

Meaning: to be busy with something

Exp: In this weekend, there is my friend's birthday, so I am tied up with my friend so I have no time. I am busy.

Dialogue:

You wanna go watch a movie?
I'd like to, but can't.
Maybe tomorrow?
I don't think I'll be able to. I'm really tied up with work these days.

*****

NO.463 - catch a movie_game

Exp: lets catch a movie or game or something else. And it means lets go to the watching movie. We use this expression in weekend when we want to do something.

Dialogue:

Yo, Pete, what's up this weekend?
Not much!
You wanna go catch a game?
Sounds great! How about tomorrow?

✱✱✱✱✱

NO.464 - to catch up

Exp: You are doing something like studying English expression and your teacher teaches 1 expression everyday and you stopped for some reason like sick. And then long time ago, you start again but now you are behind. You left lesson at 250 but now there is expression no 450, so you need to catch up. Now you will study all day and night and after one week, you cached up 450.

Dialogue:

What else we need?
Ketchup. You go down that aisle. I'll catch up with you in a minute.
But I don't know what kind of ketchup to buy.
Organic!! Duh~~

✱✱✱✱✱

NO.465 - Duh--!

Meaning: of course, why did you ask?

Exp: when somebody ask stupid question then we say Duh. For example, is Shane man?

 Duh! Of course, Shane name is male name; he is a man. Why did you ask this?

Dialogue:

So, you have an online business?

Yes. I teach online.

Oh. So, you use a computer?

Duh~~!

NO.466 - on thin ice

Meaning: in the dangers situation

Exp: if my mom is very angry at me and she is controlling herself. In this situation, I should be calm, very nice and careful. Because if I am not careful, and if I did a little noise even, she would yell at me and beat me. So I am on thin ice.

Dialogue:

Where are you?

I'm still at work.

It's 9pm!

I came in late two days in a row. I'm on thin ice here~

NO.467 - Some t-shirt, huh

Meaning: that is an amazing and wonderful

Exp: some dinner, huh; some house huh

Dialogue:

Oh, I'm full!

Me, too! Some dinner, huh?

When it comes to cooking, mom's the best.

Yes! Thanks, mom^^

NO.468 - likeminded (like-minded)

Meaning: to think the same as whatever

Exp: you and I are likeminded. And it means we think same, we have same ideas; we agree in most situations.

Dialogue:

You guys make great business partners.
You wanna know the secret?
Yeah!
We're likeminded. That's so important.

NO.469 - I need to get out more--

Meaning:

Exp: I mostly lived inside and mostly I don't go anywhere, so I need to get out more; I need to go the many place, mountain, etc.

Dialogue:

What's the last movie you saw?
In a theater? Um...oh! The Titanic. Great movie.
What? That was over 15 years ago.
Yeah... I need to get out more~

NO.470 - coming along

Meaning: progressing,

Exp: how is your dinner or proposal coming along? Is almost finish; are you progressing well; are you going better, has it been finished.

Dialogue:

How's the homework coming along?
It's almost done.
It has to be done before you meet your friends.
Don't worry. It'll be done.

*****

NO.471 - crucial

Meaning: something that is very important

Dialogue:

Cake! I'm gonna share it with Rex!
It's crucial that you don't let Rex eat this cake.
Why not? He loves all desserts.
But this is chocolate. Chocolate can kill dogs

*****

NO.472 - to breathe over someone's shoulder

Meaning: watching very closely

Exp: if somebody is breathing over your shoulder; they are watching you very closely. So its not good for you, you will not like it. Because you can't work, you can't concentrate on your work.

Dialogue:

Tim is constantly breathing over your shoulder!
I know. He's really nervous about the report.
How's it going?
It's almost finished

*****

NO.474 - a dish

Meaning: some special food that usually not serve

Exp: If you have guest in your dinner time, you will probably serve some special kind of food like vegetable dish, chicken dish, carrot dish, potato dish etc.

Dialogue:

What's that?
This is a great veggie dish to make your body stronger.
Is that kimchi? You made it?
Well, I opened the package^^

NO.475 - pizzazz

Meaning: give something extra excitement, make extra special

Exp: if you have simple T-shirt but then you add some funny text on T-shirt that is pizzazz. If you add some special food in your dish like some salad or paper, that is pizzazz.

Dialogue:

How's the stew.
It's okay. A little bland.
Argh~~ I should've added cumin.
Yeah. That would've given it some pizzazz!

NO.476 - to dabble in

Meaning: to explore, to do a little bit not professional,

Exp: I like to dabble in cooking and I am not professional cook but I like to try new cook. I checked online cooking recipes and try to make something. That's the idea of this expression.

Dialogue:

Would you help me write this sales letter?
Me? Why me?
I know you've dabbled in writing in the past.
Yeah, but that was poetry! Not business stuff!

*****

NO.477 - to be slapped with a fine

Exp: if you get a fine or some sort of penalty then you can say ' I got slapped with fine; I got slapped with penalty. Sometimes you drive fast and you may get fine or penalty.

Dialogue:

You're late.
I'm sorry. I made an illegal U-turn.
Did they let you go?
No! I got slapped with a fine.

*****

NO.479 - two-faced

Exp: if a person is very nice and polite in one situation but in other situation he is very evil. He is very opposite. He has two-faced.

Dialogue:

Oprah's on. I love her!
Turn it off.
Why? She's the greatest!
She's two-faced. On TV she seems nice, but I've heard in person...whoo!

*****

NO.480 - ticked off

Meaning: to be really angry not exploding but frustrating,

Exp: If somebody is ticking you off, they should stop make you angry otherwise you might explode.

Dialogue:

What's wrong with John?
Eric ticked him off.
Again?
Eric keeps bothering him about smoking.

NO.481 - in a rut

Exp: you go to the office daily and daily same routine makes you boring and frustrating; you can't leave because you have to make money for living. You feel like a prison so you are in a rut. Sometimes relationship may be in a rut.

Dialogue:

You don't look so happy.
I'm in a rut.
Take a break from work.
Yeah, maybe a week off would help.

NO.482 - opposites attract

Exp: men and women are opposite of each other so they attract to each other.

Dialogue:

Do you think opposites attract?
Maybe at first.
Yeah! I agree.
If two people are too different, I don't think a relationship will work

NO.483 - What keeps you up at night

Meaning: why haven't you able to sleep tonight; is there something bothering/worrying you to relaxing

Dialogue:

You always look so happy!
Yeah, thanks. But you... What keeps you up at night?
Oh, everything! My job, my bills...money!
I wish I could help~~

*****

NO.484 - a bad omen

Meaning: bad sign

Exp: if a boss or your teacher enter in the room and he is not happy, then maybe today will not good day, so you can say by looking your boss face, expression 'that's a bad omen'. This is the sign that telling you this day is not good day.

Dialogue:

It's 11 at night and still 40 out.
This is a bad omen.
I know. We're gonna die in this heat.
Thank god we have A/C.

*****

NO.485 - kerfuffle

Meaning: some craziness, a commotion

Exp: if there are many people running around and making loud voices that making problem so you would say 'what is the kerfuffle'

Dialogue:

What's all the kerfuffle about?
The lady in 407 has an alligator!
What? That's crazy!
I know, but she says it's her pet.

NO.486 - My gut tells me...

Meaning: I have a feeling inside that I think I should do this

Dialogue:

Let's go back home.
No, let's stay some more.
Two hours and not a bite.
My gut tells me the fish are getting hungry~

NO.487 - turn over a new leaf

Meaning: to turn a page on a book (2) change your life, start a new life

Exp: if you are quit smoking, you are turning over a new leaf.

Dialogue:

Is that tea?
Yeah. No more coffee for me.

You stopped drinking beer, too! Did you turn over a new leaf?
Yeah! I'm trying to be more healthy.

NO.488 - constructive criticism

Exp: if you go to the restaurant and test food that is not good, *'oh that is bad'*; if your friend make resume and you checked it, resume looks stupid, *'oh that resume is stupid'*. That is criticism that is not useful. But If you tell someone how they make it better, that is constructive criticism. You would say that food is so salty, so actually you are telling him what's the actually problem. Or you tell your friend, in resume spelling is wrong.

Dialogue:

What's wrong?
This guy said my video was bad.
Did he say why?
No! At least give me some constructive criticism if you're gonna say that~

NO.489 - Sounds about right.

Meaning: yes, I think that is correct,

Dialogue:

How much longer?
About 60 miles.
So, we should get there around 3?
Sounds about right.

NO.490 - to be after something

Meaning: to chasses something, trying to gain or get something, trying to attain something

Exp: what are you after in your life? I am after good health, dream career and dream women. So something that is your inside and you really want.

Dialogue:

What are you after in life?
Fame. I wanna be famous!
What are you after?
Money. I wanna be rich

✶✶✶✶✶

NO.491 - to gloss over something

Meaning: to give just a little bit information not in depth or in detail.

Exp: Many English teachers teach well, but they don't want to give you information in detail. So its not good. When somebody really wants to learn something they don't want to teacher gloss over. It is very common expression in advertising and marketing.

Dialogue:

Don't gloss over your pronunciation rules.
I go too quickly?
Yes. Explain them clearly.
Okay. I just thought everyone knew them.

✶✶✶✶✶

NO.492 - to be FRESH OUT OF something

Meaning: to not have anything, to have zero

Exp: I am fresh out of ideas. OR I don't have any ideas. I am fresh out of ice cream and I need to go the store.

Dialogue:

I'm going to the store.
Great. We're fresh out of milk.
Anything else?
We could use some sugar. And lettuce, too.

✱✱✱✱✱

NO.493 - I could use (something to drink_eat)

Meaning: I want to have in special meaning)

Exp: I could use a coffee. So many people drinks coffee because they just like coffee but I drink coffee because I need coffee. After drinking coffee, I become fresh and I am be able to write books. So in this case, I would say, I could use a coffee. OR I want to have coffee.

Dialogue:

Can I get you anything?
I could use a coffee.
Milk and sugar?
Black, please.

✱✱✱✱✱

NO.494 - The devil is in the details

Meaning: doing something in detail with very careful

Exp: doctor gives medicine with very carefully because if they don't, it could be dangers. Another example, accountants check their accounting with very carefully. If they want to write $ 1.0009 but if they forget to write period (.) in amount, value will be $ 10009 and it become devil and lots of financial disaster.

Dialogue:

Your scholarship application is great, but...
But what?
Pat Smith is a Mrs. not a Mr.

Oh my god...
The devil is in the details

NO.495 - Who's your money on

Meaning: who do you think would win? (if you going to do bet)

Dialogue:

The World Cup has begun!
Who's your money on?
Brazil, man. Home-field advantage.
Spain's the defending champs!

NO.496 - the refs

Dialogue:

This World Cup is gonna be hi-tech.
How so?
They're using goal-line technology.
So the refs won't miss any goals.

NO.497 - Dutch, Holland, Netherlands

Dialogue:

Where are you from?
The Netherlands.
Oh, Holland, right?
Well, Holland is actually just an area of the Netherlands.

Oh. But you're Dutch, right?
No. I'm Frisian. A different ethnic group

NO.498 - to crash (no cars!)

Meaning: extremely tired

Exp: After working, you start to crash

Dialogue:

I'm starting to crash.
How long have you been working?
I started working at 6AM. 15 hours.
Yeah. You need to get some rest, bud!

*****

NO.499 - to tear around_through

Meaning: to run really fast,

Dialogue:

What was that?
The cat's tearing around the house.
He broke my lamp!
But he's so cute^

*****

NO.500 - to be STOKED (ending conversation fixed!)

Meaning: excited, very enthusiastic,

Exp: I am very stoked to writing books.

Dialogue:

Wow! 500 E-cubed lessons!
That's a lot, huh?
Yes! You must be exhausted!
No way! I'm stoked! 500 more!

NO.501 - dead broke

Meaning: to really have no money, zero money,

Dialogue:

Did you hear what Hillary Clinton said?
Now what?
After Bill retired as president, they were dead broke!
What? Dead broke! Tell her to come live with us! She'll see dead broke!

NO.503 - to bow out

Meaning: to quit something but by showing respect

Dialogue:

I heard your marathon is tomorrow.
Yeah, but I had to bow out.
What? Why?
My knee went out. I can't run.

NO.504 - pass it on/along

Meaning: to continue to pass something, to continue to spread information, secret or object

Exp: you download my book, and then pass it on OR give it your friend; share with your friends.

Dialogue:

Hey, Brian's birthday is Friday.
Oh.
We're gonna have a surprise birthday party for him. Pass it along.
You bet.

NO.505 - Mum's the word

Meaning: don't say anything,

Exp: if anybody asked you, you just say 'I don't know'

Dialogue:

We're having a surprise birthday party for Brian on Friday.
Awesome.
Mum's the word, okay?
Got it

NO.506 - my lips are sealed

Meaning: mum's the word, you can't tell anything what you know

Dialogue:

Ryan's birthday party is Friday. It's a secret.
You mean Brian?
Oh, yeah. Brian. It's a secret.
My lips are sealed.

*****

NO.507 - a nail-biter

Meaning: something that make you really nerves, really scared, really anxious

Exp: sometime you watch sports game, and both teams are tough, and any team can win so that game is a nail-biter.

Dialogue:

Did you see the Greece-Ivory Coast match?
Yes!
That was a nail-biter!
I'm loving these lesser-known teams!

*****

NO.508 - You name it

Meaning: you decide, its up to you,

Exp: you are your friend are going to a restaurant and your friend ask you ' what should we eat?', you could say ' you name it' OR you decide; I can eat everything that you decide or suggest.

Dialogue:

You wanna name my cat?
No! You name it!
What should I name it?
You name it!
How about...Shane?

*****

NO.509 - to feign something

Meaning: to pretend, acting,

Dialogue:

Here comes the boss.
He saw us watching the game.
Quick--feign death.
Were you men watching the game? Guys? Sue, bring my gun. Let's make sure they're dead.

NO.510 - take a dip

Meaning: to get into the swimming pool,

Dialogue:

It's so hot.
Let's go take a dip.
Great idea! The lake?
Too far. Let's go to the pool.

NO.511 - to talk a mile a minute

Meaning: to talk really fast,

Dialogue:

Did you understand anything he said?
No! He talks a mile a minute~
He should be a sports announcer!
Yeah! He'd be perfect for the World Cup^^

NO.512 - a poor excuse

Meaning: lie,

Dialogue:

He broke up with you? Why?
He said, "You're too good for me."
Oh~ That's a poor excuse! He has a woman!!
I know~ He's such a loser~~

✽✽✽✽✽

NO.513 - out of date

Meaning: old fashioned,

Dialogue:

What are you doing?
I'm updating the software. It's out of date.
Oh, I should do that, too.
I'll let you know if it's any good

✽✽✽✽✽

NO.514 - a bug (bugs)

Meaning: problem

Exp: if you upgrade your computer or software but they doesn't work because of bug OR they have some problem.

Dialogue:

So, how's the update?
There's a major bug!

What?
My battery life was cut in half! I switched back to the old system

NO.515 - a bug (RARELY plural)

Dialogue:

Wash your hands with soap.
Alright~~
There's a bug going around.
Okay!

NO.516 -but no---

Dialogue:

Want some more vegetables?
No! I could have been having a barbecue, but no~~~
Quit complaining. The rain is nice!
I wanted hamburgers!!!

*****

NO.517 - cry me a river

Meaning: go ahead and cry but I don't care

Exp: we use this expression when we were angry on somebody.

Dialogue:

Paris was wonderful but the wine was so expensive.
Uh-huh.

Really. We paid over 100 euros every night for dinner.
Cry me a river~~

NO.518 - weather VS climate

__Meaning__: weather is short term but climate is a long term

__Dialogue:__

How's the weather today?
It's raining! It's great!
I thought it never rained there.
Rarely. The climate here is really dry!

NO.519 - What the

__Exp__: actually we are missing word, what the hell; what the hack. You are angry and you want to say what's going on.

__Dialogue:__

What the...
What's wrong?
The bank charged me a fee for putting money in my account!
What? Are you serious?

NO.520 - in a nutshell

__Meaning__: in short and simple words,

__Dialogue:__

Do you think I can use this song in my YouTube video?
Well, the copyright laws are very strict.
And complicated.
Yeah. But in a nutshell, if you didn't make it, don't use it

NO.521 - heading VS going

Meaning: both words has same meaning

Dialogue:

Going somewhere?
I'm heading out.
Where you going?
I'll head over to Mike's then home.

NO.522 - Will do

Meaning: ok, I will do it,

Exp: if somebody ask to you to do something, you would say ' will do'

Dialogue:

You going over to Mike's?
Yeah. I'm on my way now.
Tell him I'll see him on Friday.
Will do.

NO.523 - to put lipstick on a pig

Meaning: something is really bad but we try to make it really nice it is the same as putting lipstick on a pig.

Exp: if there is a some ugly building in your neighborhood and they painted for looking good but building is still ugly, so that's like putting lipstick on a pig.

Dialogue:

What do you think of my business proposal?
Well, I don't think it'll work.
What if I add more graphs and pictures?
That's just putting lipstick on a pig! Sorry

✳✳✳✳✳

NO.524 - What's all this RACKET!

Meaning: what's all this noise?

Exp: Usually when we are not happy then we use this expression. If we are studying and there is some children making noise, so you will be unable to concentrate your study then you become angry and would say' what's all this racket.'

Dialogue:

What's all this racket?
I'm trying to fix the sink.
It sounds like your destroying it.
Then YOU do it!

✳✳✳✳✳

NO.525 - cut to the chase

Meaning: don't tell the useless stuff and come to the point

Dialogue:

Go ahead.
Well, you know how I love you. And I think you're the greatest...
Cut to the chase!
Can I get 20 dollars?

*****

NO.526 - fingers crossed

Meaning: let's hope for best, let's be hopeful, (2) also use this expression in negative meaning

Dialogue:

John failed his exam.
Ha! I'm glad. He never studied.
But you told him you would keep your fingers crossed for him.
Yeah, but I crossed my fingers on my other hand when I said it!

*****

NO.527 - leave no stone unturned

Meaning: to look everywhere, search everywhere

Exp: I lose my house key many times, so I leave no stone unturned. I looked everywhere for find my keys in refrigerator, bed, table and everywhere.

Dialogue:

Did you find them yet?
No. I'm still looking.
Leave no stone unturned. I need them!
How can anyone lose their glasses?!!

*****

NO.528 - travel halfway around the world to

Meaning: want to really to do something, would do everything to do something

Exp: I have fantastic girl in my life but we are separated right now, and I would do everything to be her.

Dialogue:

I'd travel halfway around the world to meet Celine Dion.
She lives about 10 miles from you.
Yeah, but she'd never meet me~
True~ But I'm sure "your heart will go on!

NO.529 - Blah-

Meaning: so so, terrible, I don't know, bored, tired, no energy,

Exp: so if you have no energy in your life and your life is boring and somebody ask you ' hay , how you doing?' you would say 'blah'

Dialogue:

You look a little...
Blah?
Yeah!
I'm am blah~ Nothing's going right in my life~

NO.530 - gives me a complex

Meaning: it makes me feel inferior,

Exp: When I am lonely, I feel confident but when he comes to my home, suddenly, I feel that I am nothing and I am stupid and he is star and genius. So he gives me a complex.

Dialogue:

Let's go to John's barbecue this Sunday.
No. He gives me a complex.
What? Why?
His life is so perfect. My life is so blah~

NO.531 - peachy (RE-DONE!)

Meaning: great,

Exp: how is your day today? Its peachy OR its great and very nice. This word is opposite of word 'blah.'

Dialogue:

Hi! Long time no see!
Yeah, good to see you! How's everything?
Everything's peachy! Yourself?
Couldn't be better!

NO.532 - to FOLLOW ALONG

Meaning: to listen carefully so that you understand,

Dialogue:

The first thing you need to do is call the US embassy.
That's the first thing?
Weren't you following along? That's what the travel office said.
Oh, I guess just looking at the pictures on the wall

NO.533 - sob VS wail VS whimper

Meaning: sob: very wet cry(little kids cry like this), wail: cry very loudly, whimper: (animals or girlfriend are the example of the whimper crying

Dialogue:

When I saw that puppy whimpering I wanted to cry.
I was completely sobbing. It was so sad.
I'm glad mom didn't see it.
I know! She would have been wailing!!

NO.534 - discipline (noun and verb)

Meaning: manners, **as a verb**: punish in order to gain control or enforce obedience

Dialogue:

Ooh! Cake! Maybe I'll get a small piece.
Aren't you on a diet? You need some discipline.
Who's gonna discipline me?
Me!! Ha! I brought a mirror! Look at yourself!

NO.535 - a longshot

Meaning: unlikely happening ,

Exp: speaking English like a native English speaker is a longshot.

Dialogue:

Do you think Shane will become a Hollywood movie star?
It's a longshot!
Really? I think he's SO talented.
Yeah, but he's bald! And old!

* * * * *

NO.537 - hand-me-downs

Exp: clothes that your elder brother used to, but now he is to big so now you wear it. So you are using used clothing that used to worn by your brother. These clothes called hand-me-downs.

Dialogue:

Your throwing away all those clothes?
Yeah. They're hand-me-downs.
Let me see them. I'll take some of these!
Help yourself. They were my uncle's

* * * * *

NO.538 - a no-brainer

Meaning: obvious,

Exp: if something is a no-brainer, it is a decision that you make which does not require your brain. So I am going to desert and I think myself 'should I take some water with me?' that's a no-brainer. You don't have to think about it. If you go to the desert, of course you need to water. That's a stupid question.

Dialogue:

My English is good, but I can't hear what native speakers say!
Yes. That's why I joined DDM. It was a no-brainer.
Has it helped?
Are you joking?! I've improved SO much!

* * * * *

NO.539 - a dead giveaway

Meaning: something completely obvious, obvious clew,

Exp: do you think Shane is American or British. You can tell this just by hearing him pronunciation. So pronunciation is a dead giveaway.

Dialogue:

So, did you like the chocolate cake?
Huh? Oh...how'd you know I ate some?
Well, the chocolate all over your teeth was a dead giveaway.
Ugh~

✳✳✳✳✳

NO.540 - cut through the clutter

Meaning: standing

Exp: There are many YouTube English teachers and now you want to teach English and want that everyone can see you. So it's not easy, OR it's very difficult to cut through the clutter.

Dialogue:

What's this?
That's my resume.
It's pink. A pink resume?
Yes! I gotta cut through the clutter

✳✳✳✳✳

NO.541 - thrift shop

Meaning: shop where you can buy really cheap used clothes, toys and anything used,

Dialogue:

New shirt?
Yep.
Thrift shop?

How'd you know?
Just a guess.

✱✱✱✱✱

NO.542 - kick off

Meaning: to start something,

Dialogue:

When's the season kick off?
Football?
Is there another season?
September 4th

✱✱✱✱✱

NO.543 - to PICK it UP (3 meanings!)

Meaning: (1)to pick something like pen/marker, (2)to clean like your room, (3)go faster, increase your speed,

Exp: pick up your room,

Dialogue:

Coach Shane speaks to slow.
You think so?
Yes. I wish he'd pick it up!
Leave him a message.

✱✱✱✱✱

NO.544 - to be GIFTED

Meaning: very smart and talented,

Dialogue:

What are you gifted at?
Sleeping!
No, serious. Tell me!
Hmm... I guess I'm a very good explainer!

＊＊＊＊＊

NO.545 - mental

Meaning: stupid

Dialogue:

Where are you going?
I'm gonna go play golf.
Golf is so mental.
No, it's not. But it is a very mental game.

＊＊＊＊＊

NO.546 - short and sweet

Meaning: it was short and it does not required much time

Exp: how was the movie? Short and sweet

Dialogue:

Oh, you're finished with the book?
Yep. You wanna read it?
Maybe. How was it?
Short and sweet. You'll like it.

＊＊＊＊＊

NO.548 - let it slide

Meaning: it's no big deal, forget about it,

Dialogue:

I'm surprised to see you here.
Why?
Your mom was SO mad at you the other day.
Oh, she always lets me slide! I'm her angel^^

NO.549 - for starters

Meaning: in the beginning, the first thing,

Dialogue:

My English isn't improving.
How are you studying?
Books. Sometimes movies.
Well, for starters, you should be watching E-cubed every day!

NO.550 - to patch things up

Meaning: to resolve a problem especially in relationship,

Dialogue:

Come to the game with us!
You and Sue are back together?
Yeah! We patched things up.
That's great! We'll join you!

✱✱✱✱✱

NO.551 - to chime in

Meaning: to give idea or suggestion, (2) to interrupt

Exp: when I am speaking, don't chime in OR don't speak and don't add your comments

Dialogue:

I completely disagreed with John.
Really?
Yes! He was totally wrong.
Why didn't you chime in

✱✱✱✱✱

NO.552 - to be long-winded

Meaning: describe somebody who talks and talks a lot

Exp: if somebody is long-winder, you will probably say ' shut up, please stop'. Do you long-winded?

Dialogue:

Are you watching C-Span?
Yeah.
Those guys are so long-winded. How can you watch?
It helps me fall asleep!

✱✱✱✱✱

NO.554 - lemming, sheep, sheeple

Meaning: mindless person called lemming, sheep or sheeple

Exp: Lemming, sheep or sheeple are same thing and these types of People don't used their head and always follow to others. If somebody tells him to buy some product for good-looking, they would mindlessly follow them and buy product. For example, lemming person said *"hay, I want to lose weight'* the other said *' ok, just eat water melon a lot'* and then lemming person start to eat water melon without thinking, *'oh, I am losing weight because I am eating water melon.'*

Dialogue:

Dude, your phone is so old.
It still works.
And when's the last time you bought clothes?
I don't need any.
Come on!
Hey, I'm not a lemming! I do things my own way

✳✳✳✳✳

NO.555 - to eyeball something

Meaning: to look at something, judging it,

Dialogue:

How many boxes are you going to need?
I have no idea.
Just eyeball your stuff and guess.
Um…twelve, maybe.

✳✳✳✳✳

NO.556 - in a huff

Meaning: angrily,

Exp: we walked away in a huff.

Dialogue:

Where's Shane going in a huff?
He's mad again.
What'd you do?
I told him his jokes weren't funny.

✱✱✱✱✱

NO.557 - a knee-jerk reaction/response

Meaning: automatically, without thinking,

Exp: if somebody yell at you *'shut up, be quite'* and you probably would say without *thinking ' you shut up'* but later you realized that it was your mom. *'oh sorry mom'*. That was your knee-jerk reaction.

Dialogue:

What do you think of the riots?
Well, my knee-jerk reaction is to support the people.
But?
But, after I thought about it, violence with violence never solves anything.

✱✱✱✱✱

NO.558 - drained

Meaning: energy is gone,

Exp: if we worked very hard all day, we will say *'I am drained'*. It may be physically drained and it also may be mentally drained.

Dialogue:

You look tired.
I'm totally drained.
What happened?
Eh~ Some people expect too much.

*****

NO.559 - buff

Meaning: heavy good solid muscle especially arms

Exp: some people exercise to be buff. I am not buff.

Dialogue:

You're pretty buff.
Yeah? I've been working out a bit.
Great! Any reason?
Not really. I just like the exercise.

*****

NO.560 - Yes siree, Bob!

Meaning: absolutely,

Dialogue:

I'd like to upgrade my internet speed to Ultra.
No problem.
Can you come out with the new modem tomorrow?
Yes, siree, Bob!

*****

NO.561 - lean on me

Meaning: grab somebody when you feeling difficulties,

Dialogue:

I'm so nervous. Moving to another country.
Well, lean on me. I'm there for you.

45

I really appreciate it.
Hey, that's what friends are for

NO.562 - sound asleep

Meaning: sleeping very deeply,

Exp: if somebody sound asleep, they will not wake up even someone is screaming, noising etc.

Dialogue:

Where were you last night?
I went to bed early. I was tired~
I called you three times!
Sorry~ I was sound asleep!

NO.563 - Lay it on me!

Meaning: tell me,

Exp: We use this expression in situation when somebody wants to tell you some important thing. So when you say 'lat it on me' that means you are completely focus on person that want to tell you something. If you are busy and working, then you would say ' I am busy right now' but later when you have done then you can say ' you wanted to tell me something important, so now I can hear you and can help you OR lay it on me.

Dialogue:

Do you have time now?
Oh, right. Your new idea. Lay it on me.
Well, I think you should make a better website.
Ugh! I know! It's urgent~~

NO.564 - under my belt

Meaning: to gain some special experience, you have knowledge in something and now you can move something else,

Dialogue:

I'm a beginner, but can I join DDM?
Well, once you get my Daily Dictation videos under your belt, then you can join.
How much are those lessons?
How much? They're free!

NO.565 - pull your weight

Meaning: do your job, take care your responsibility,

Dialogue:

Oh, no. Is John on our team?
Yeah, why?
He never pulls his weight!
Really? He seems like a hard worker

NO.566 - flickering

Meaning: lights that almost dead,

Exp: lights become dark and light, dark and light before die. That's flickering.

Dialogue:

Do you have a minute?
What do you need?

The light in my room is flickering.
I'll change it for you.

NO.567 - Dork

Meaning: somebody who is weird and silly,

Dialogue:

What are you doing?
Oh…just…nothing.
Making faces in the mirror? Dork!
Leave me alone~

NO.568 - urbanite

Meaning: opposite of dork, person who love city and attractive style,

Dialogue:

Let's go to Le Grange tonight!
The restaurant? No thanks~
Why not? It sounds great~
Pfft~ It's for urbanites!

NO.569 - farm-to-fork

Meaning: foods that produced locally,

Exp: some grocery store contract to a farm directly for food like milk, beef and others.

Dialogue:

What are your grocery bills?
A little high. About $300.
Wow! Why so much?
I look for farm-to-fork foods. They're pricier.

✱✱✱✱✱

NO.570 - rat's nest

Meaning: messy,

Exp: your room is rats' nest OR your room is messy.

Dialogue:

I have to go to Eduardo's today.
You don't sound too excited.
No, his place is a rat's nest. Yuck~
It can't be that bad!

✱✱✱✱✱

NO.571 - Don't quit your day job!

Meaning: regular job, main job

Exp: Shane day job is English coach, and he are saying that he is quite this job in future and start another job. So you can say to shane ' don't quit your day job!'

Dialogue:

I started a new business!
Doing what?
I'm gonna sell handmade wool socks!
In the desert? Don't quit your day job!

✱✱✱✱✱

NO.572 - sugarcoat

Meaning: lie,

Dialogue:

So, how'd you like my poem?
Well...it was nice.
Come on! Don't sugarcoat it! Tell me.
Um... Don't quit your day job.

NO.573 - grab a nap

Meaning: sleep

Exp: I like to grab a nap after lunch.

Dialogue:

Is there anything else you need?
No, nothing. Thanks.
Okay. I'm gonna go grab a nap.
Sleep well^^

NO.574 - don't quote me on that

Meaning: I am not exactly sure, it might be wrong (2) don't tell anyone that I said

Dialogue:

Coach Shane's starting a new class next month, but don't quote me on that.
Cool! What kind?
For speaking. Very necessary.
Excellent. I'm gonna sign up!

*****

NO.575 - to be chummy with

Meaning: to be very close, to be very nice someone,

Exp: don't' be chummy with someone in order to get something. It's not nice.

Dialogue:

Why are you being all chummy with Lima?
You don't know?
Don't know what?
He's one of the owners of Manchester United!

*****

NO.575 - to be chummy with

Meaning: to be very close, to be very nice someone,

Exp: don't' be chummy with someone in order to get something. It's not nice.

Dialogue:

Why are you being all chummy with Lima?
You don't know?
Don't know what?
He's one of the owners of Manchester United!

*****

NO.576 - give him the benefit of the doubt

Exp: if someone tells you some truth, but you don't 100% believe them. Actually you like to more information or proof. Maybe this person, in the past, has lied to you before. But anyway you say 'ok, I accept what you say as the truth'. So you doubt, you don't really believe. And benefit, you are giving him a benefit that you will believe now. Later you might be angry when you get know that this person is wrong but now you believe.

Dialogue:

Where's Mark? He's late.
He said he got a flat tire.
And you believed him.
Let's give him the benefit of the doubt

✱✱✱✱✱

NO.577 - Holy crap!

Meaning: oh my God, What the, really, Wow!!,

Dialogue:

Holy crap!
What? What happened?
I just put vinegar in the cake mix.
You idiot! You fool! Ugh

✱✱✱✱✱

NO.578 - I lost my cool!

Exp: if someone really get angry, they shout, they throw things at you then we say ' he lost his cool'

Dialogue:

Why is there spaghetti sauce on the wall?
Oh...I got a little angry last night...
And?
And I lost my cool. I'll clean it up.

✱✱✱✱✱

NO.579 - Have a go!

Meaning: give it try, try it once, go for it,

Dialogue:

You look like you need help.
Well, I'm trying to decide if I should try DDM.
Have a go! I think you'd like it!
But I'm too old~~

✶✶✶✶✶

NO.580 - What gives-

Meaning: what's deal

Exp: we use this expression when we angry on someone like singer justin has quit singing. "what gives".

Dialogue:

I heard you told everyone I failed the test.
Well, I...
What gives? Huh?
I just didn't want people to bother you

✶✶✶✶✶

NO.581 - a rubbernecker

Meaning: distracted,

Dialogue:

Oh no. Be careful. An accident.
Whoa! On the other side of the street, too!

Don't be a rubbernecker.
Don't worry. My eyes are on the road.

NO.582 - count your blessings

Meaning: remember your blessings,

Exp: if you speak English, you are lucky because you can go anywhere and easily communicate with anybody. Count your blessings. You are lucky.

Dialogue:

Are you crying?
No, I'm just so sad for the children.
Yeah... War is so disgusting.
I count my blessings every day.

NO.583 - Close, but no cigar

Meaning: you are almost correct but not 100% right,

Exp: what is my age? "20" No. "27". Oh yes, close but no cigar. I am 28.

Dialogue:

How many states in the United States of America?
48!
Wrong.
54.
Wrong.
51!
Close, but no cigar! 50 is the right answer

*****

NO.584 - snazzy

Meaning: looks really nice, special and cool

Dialogue:

Did you see Pavel's team photo?
The soccer team photo?
Yeah! Pretty snazzy uniforms!
But can they play?!

*****

NO.585 - chintzy

Meaning: cheap,

Exp: if someone wants to give me tea. Don't be chintzy. Give me a lot

Dialogue:

I'll give you 50 cents each time you take out the garbage.
What?! Don't be so chintzy, dad!
Whoa! My dad gave me 50 cents, so I'm giving you 50 cents.
Dad, that was like 50 years ago!!

*****

NO.586 - to move mountains

Dialogue:

Your daughter works so hard.
I know. Her determination is amazing.
She'll move mountains one day!
She just might!

✻✻✻✻✻

NO.587 - to freeze my butt off

Meaning: super cold

Dialogue:

I heard you're moving to the mountains.
That's the plan.
You're gonna freeze your butt off!
Better than melting!

✻✻✻✻✻

NO.588 - to ace something

Meaning: to score perfectly.

Exp: if you take test in your school and you grade A+. really high score. Did you ace your test in your class.

Dialogue:

So, how was the driver's test?
I aced it!
Really?
Well, I got one wrong out of 50!

✻✻✻✻✻

NO.589 - itching to do something

Meaning: really want to do something,

Dialogue:

I'm itching to go to the mountains.
What for?
Just to be in nature. To be around trees!
What are you? A bear?!!

NO.590 - to go pear-shaped

Dialogue:

I know!! I'm totally pear-shaped!
Your diet didn't work?
My diet went pear-shaped from day one~

NO.591 - to cut it close

Meaning: very very close, to almost miss something,

Dialogue:

There! Just in time.
We have two minutes.
Just in time!!
We cut it close. Let's get here earlier tomorrow, please.

NO.593 - to kill two birds with one stone

Meaning: getting two things done in one stroke,

Exp: if I am about to go to the grocery store to buy milk. And my mom said to me to check mail box. So I am getting two things done in one way.

Dialogue:

I wanna cook beef tonight.
Look up a recipe with buttermilk.
What? Why?
This buttermilk is going to expire, so if you can use it in a beef recipe you'll be killing two birds with one stone!

NO.594 - to harbor a feeling of (anger, jealousy, or anxiety)

Exp: if you look normal in outside but inside, you are feeling anger, jealousy, or anxiety, You are keeping your feeling inside and you are not telling or showing anyone your anger feeling.

Dialogue:

Look at that guy~ Oh, I have a Porsche~~
You seem to harbor a lot of hatred for rich people.
No, just rich people who didn't earn their money.
How do you know how he got his money?

NO.595 - tit for tat

Exp: if you hit me I will hit you. If you say something bad me, I will say you bad.

Dialogue:

The US is angry at Russia so it wants to block Russian products.
Russia might just do the same.
Tit for tat~
Kids

NO.596 - man the grill

Meaning: to operate something, to handle something,

Exp: who is going to cooking today in restaurant.

Dialogue:

What's that?
Leftover hamburgers! They're from the barbecue last night.
They look perfect. Who manned the grill?
Shane, of course!

✳✳✳✳✳

NO.597 - I have a penchant for

Meaning: really like something and cannot resist something, (especially for food)

Exp: I have a penchant for fried chicken.

Dialogue:

What's Shane doing?
He's making homemade caramel for his coffee!
Wow! He made fudge brownies the other day.
He has a penchant for sweet things!!

✳✳✳✳✳

NO.598 - to tie one on

Meaning: to drink a lot alcohol,

Dialogue:

You look horrible.
Well, I feel horrible.

You tied one on last night, didn't you?
Oh yea

NO.599 - I was conned into VERB ing

Meaning: to be tricked, to be deceived,

Dialogue:

Ten dollars to park?
Yeah! I was conned into paying it!
How so?
The guy told me there was no other place to park without getting a ticket. He totally lied to me.

NO.600 - a sub _ to sub for

Meaning: to substitute,

Exp: if I am busy this month so I am not going to write a new book, would you sub for me OR would write book for me. If you do, Thank you.

Dialogue:

I'm heading to the mountains tomorrow.
But what about your classes?
I'm getting a sub.
Can I do it? Please?

NO.601 - the nitty-gritty

Meaning: real find detail, very specific information,

Dialogue:

I wish Coach Shane would teach more about pronunciation.
He does in DDM and PIRF. He really gets into the nitty-gritty.
But I don't have any money.
Investment in knowledge pays the best interest.

✻✻✻✻✻

NO.602 - a hollow victory

Meaning: empty victory,

Dialogue:

Germany killed Brazil in the World Cup.
Yeah, but it was a hollow victory.
How so? It was awesome!
Yeah, but Brazil was without their number one player~

✻✻✻✻✻

NO.603 - lock, stock and barrel

Meaning: everything,

Exp: Did you put everything in car. Yes lock, stock and barrel OR everything.

Dialogue:

Did you pack everything?
Lock, stock and barrel.
Great. Let's go!!
Wait~ Where are the keys?

✻✻✻✻✻

NO.604 - the lowdown

Meaning: real important fundamental information but not necessary nitty gritty,

Exp: when you sign a contract, like buying a car, contract describes everything but each of the points is the lowdown.

Dialogue:

Where can I get the lowdown on DDM LITE?
He's got a webpage: www.letsmasterenglish.com/ddmlite
That page has all the info I need?
Everything.

NO.605 - give him an inch and he'll take a mile

Meaning: very greedy,

Dialogue:

Shane, can I borrow your car this weekend?
Okay. But don't go too far.
Don't worry! Thanks!! And please make sure the tank is full!! Bye~
What?!! Give him an inch and he'll take a mile!

NO.606 - Watch your step!

Meaning: be careful,

Dialogue:

Let's hurry! I don't want to be late.
Okay! Hey, watch your step~~

Oh...gross!! Gum!!!
I told you to watch your step~~

NO.607 - to drop off and drop-off

Meaning: to put something, to leave something at somewhere,

Exp: if you are in a taxi, *"can you drop off at this point."*

Dialogue:

Drop me off over here.
I dropped off Lucas here, too!
It's the best drop-off point for subway and bus users.
I see. Watch your step as you get out--there's quite a drop-off

✳✳✳✳✳

NO.608 - Honest to a fault

Meaning: too honest,

Exp: When mother cooks something we should not criticize her; we always should say that it is delicious. To criticize on their mother is not a good thing. But when my mother cooks something and if there is not delicious. I say "mom, it is not delicious because it is too salty." So I am being too honest. I am honest to fault OR I am too honest. It is not good, because sometimes we should speak white lie.

Dialogue:

Jim's so honest! He just turned in a wallet full of cash!
I hate Jim.
What? He's a great guy.
Really? He told me yesterday I was gaining weight!
Well...I guess he's just honest to a fault!

✳✳✳✳✳

NO.609 - you are smarter than he looks

Meaning: you looks stupid but actually you are very intelligent,

Dialogue:

Why didn't you tell your mom where you were?
Because she would have worried too much!
Wow! You're smarter than you look!
Thanks, dad! Let's enjoy the game^

✳✳✳✳✳

NO.610 - Give credit where credit is due

Meaning: thank very much but I also want to thank this person, don't give me all credit we also give credit to this person too,

Exp: If you made a soup in a dinner party. And in making this soup, there was another person with you. And everyone said to you that soup was very good. So you can say "thank you, but let's give credit where credit is due.. his person." OR This person also helps me to making this soup.

Dialogue:

In British pronunciation they say "better", but in American pronunciation they say "better".
Hey, your English pronunciation has really improved!
Well, it's thanks to you, Coach Shane.
A little maybe, but let's give credit where credit is due—you worked HARD!

✳✳✳✳✳

NO.611 - wrapped around someone's finger

Meaning: to control someone completely,

64

Exp: He is controlling her. And what he said to her, she does.

Dialogue:

What are you doing? Grocery shopping?
Yeah.
She's got you wrapped around her finger.
I do it because I love her.

NO.612 - to feel a little warm

Meaning: start to feel sick, fever,

Dialogue:

Ugh~~
You don't look good.
I feel a little warm.
Let's take your temperature.

NO.613 - nauseous

Meaning: feeling sick in your stomach like vomit,

Exp: I am feeling nauseous. Sometime when eat something that is not good, you feel nauseous.

Dialogue:

You okay?
I'm feeling a bit nauseous.
Have you thrown up?
No, but I think I might.

NO.614 - the runs

Exp: Sometimes you eat something wrong, and you need to go the bathroom urgently. And you run to the bathroom quickly. For this situation you can use this expression.

Dialogue:

I don't think I can go in today.
What's wrong?
My stomach. I've got the runs.
I'll call your boss. Turn the fan on.

NO.615 - freeloader

Exp: children are freeloader. They take your food and take things and take every time and never gives. They like to get thing for free.

Dialogue:

Why do you let Freddie just eat your food?
I don't know. He doesn't eat much.
He's a freeloader.
He's my brother! Let him be~~

NO.617 - Tupperware

Meaning: any type of container that you can put food into,

Dialogue:

More Tupperware?
My mom's got tons.
You reuse it, right?
Sure! Well, I bring the dirty ones back to her.

*****

NO.619 - an old-timer

Meaning: for a longtime, (2) if someone is lot of experience in one area called an old-timer

Dialogue:

When did you start teaching on YouTube?
Back in 2010.
Oh, so you're an old-timer.
Not really, a few go back to 2006.

*****

NO.620 - a show of hands

Meaning: display hands,

Exp: If five people are sitting there, and I asked them "let me see a show of hand who like pizza" . And one person show his hand and said "I like pizaa"

Dialogue:

With a show of hands, how many of you like English?
Excellent! How many of you know Coach Shane?
Wow! Everyone?
Of course...YOU are Coach Shane! Duh~~

*****

NO.621 - dinner and a movie

Meaning: simple and clean date(first time)

Exp: In this situation, if a man see a women and want to have date her, so he asked her "how about dinner and a movie.

67

Dialogue:

it's been really nice talking to you.
Me, too. Enjoy your stay in New York.
I will. Um, if you have time, how about dinner and a movie?
That sounds lovely. Um, let me ask my husband...

NO.622 - skip the middleman

Dialogue:

Nice cup. Where'd you get it?
Amazon.
Look, it's made here in town!
Really? Aw~ I should've skipped the middleman!

NO.624 - to josh someone

Meaning: to tease,

Dialogue:

Coach Shane received Halloween candy today!
What? Are you joshing me?
No. He went as a cowboy and got lots of candy~
But Halloween's for children~ Oh my god!

NO.625 - earnest

Meaning: hardworking and series,

Exp: You guys are very earnest in studying English. You are very mature about study.

Dialogue:

What's so funny?
My English lesson!
I thought you were a serious student—no time for fun.
I am an earnest student. Serious does not have to equal boring.

NO.626 - What a joke-

Meaning: oh my God and I can't believe that, that is terrible and ridicules, what is that,

Dialogue:

What a joke.
What?
President Obama's Press Secretary's name is Josh Earnest.
Yeah, so?
Josh—to lie. Earnest—very serious. So...he's a serious liar.
Yeah~ What a joke!

NO.627 - Get the vote out!

Meaning: get out there and vote,

Dialogue:

Did you vote?
No.
Why not? Get the vote out!
It doesn't matter.
Yes it does! Polls are closing! GO!

NO.628 - a rain check

Exp: I went to the store for buying chicken because it was cheap. But he said that he was completely sold out chicken but he will give me a rain check. And then, he gave me a coupon, so that I can come back in week for chicken. That was a rain check.

Dialogue:

Wanna go to the baseball game tonight with me?
I thought you went yesterday.
It rained—they gave me a rain check.
Oh~ Can I get a rain check, too? I have to work late.

*****

NO.629 - use your noggin

Meaning: use your head, think about and solve the problem, use your intellect,

Exp: Somebody has problem and he said that how could he solve the problem. "use your noggin" OR use your head

Dialogue:

How can crack open this walnut?
Use your noggin!
Oh, okay. OW!!
NO!! Use your brains, silly!

*****

NO.630 - put a dent into something

Exp: If you have a lot of work and you are doing but nobody can see your work. And you need to do more work hard, so that everybody can see. You need to put a dent. For example, I buy a huge book about 4000 page, and in three days, I read 300 pages. So you cannot see that I read. So I need to read at least 2000 pages more, so that you can see that I have read. Otherwise you will say to me that I done nothing.

Dialogue:

I made this cake for my mom yesterday, but she didn't even put a dent into it.
Awesome! Let's dig in!
Don't you want a plate?
No need!!

✱✱✱✱✱

NO.631 - eats like a bird!

Meaning: eats a little bit,

Exp: you are eating like a bird, OR you eat a small bite in bread or something other food.

Dialogue:

That was SO good. Your mom doesn't like cake?
No, she loves it.
Then why didn't she eat it?
She did, it's just that she eats like a bird!

✱✱✱✱✱

NO.632 - to be ON THE LEVEL WITH someone

Meaning: talking straight, being honest,

Exp: Be honest and share all information with someone that you know. That is the expression means.

Dialogue:

You voted for him? I thought you liked the other guy.
I did, but I just don't think he's on the level with the public.

Are any politicians on the level with us?
Maybe not, but I think this guy's better~

NO.633 - chitchat VS shoot the breeze

Dialogue:

Where were you? It's 9!
Shooting the breeze with Bill.
I thought you said men don't chitchat.
We don't. We shoot the breeze. Sports. Hunting. Fishing.

NO.634 - Don't knock it 'til you try it!

Meaning: don't criticize before you try,

Exp: if you don't know about something, don't criticize about it. And don't say any negative.

Dialogue:

What'd you eat for lunch, Coach Shane?
I ate one of my cat's ears.
I don't like cats.
Wellington, don't knock it 'til you try it!

*****

NO.635 - I misspoke-

Dialogue:

You ate "mousse kaka" and your cat's ear?
Well, I just bit my cat's ear, I didn't really eat it!

Hm-hmm. And "mousse kaka"?
I totally misspoke! It's moussaka! I'm so sorry to EVERY Greek food love

NO.636 - AWOL

Meaning: absent without leave(military expression)

Dialogue:

Uh…where's Pavel? He should be here.
He went AWOL.
Isn't tonight the Banda MS concert?
That's right! He's in the band!! Arriba, arriba! Andale, andale! (Get up! Let's go!)

NO.638 - inscribe

Meaning: inscribe: carve, cut, or etch into a material or surface,

Dialogue:

Did you inscribe Coach Shane?
Where?
On the internet. His YouTube channel.
You mean SUBSCRIBE! Yes^^
Inscribe, subscribe! What's the difference?!
This…

*****

NO.639 - to leave one's mark

Dialogue:

I'm leaving my mark on this rock.
For what?
So that people will know that I was here!
With watercolor paint?

NO.640 - bacon

Meaning: family money,

Exp: that money is pay for rent, electricity, called bacon money

Dialogue:

What's that smell?
I'm making bacon.
It's not breakfast!
It's for my video. I'm making bacon to make the bacon.

NO.641 - earthy colors_tones

Meaning: mix of brown, greens colors like earth color

Dialogue:

What'd you get me? A dress?
Yep! In your favorite color, too!
Let me see! Oh~ Brown, huh? You have the receipt?
What? I thought you liked earthy colors~~

NO.643 - a loud tie

Meaning: too bright color of something,

Dialogue:

Um…where are you going with that tie?
My interview. I've got to look unique.
Yeah, but that tie is way too loud. Try this.
Green? Boring

✳✳✳✳✳

NO.644 - I owe it all to… (Thanksgiving Special)

Meaning: I need to thank you

Dialogue:

You are looking good today!
I owe it all to my barber.
Yeah! What a great cut~
My barber's the best!

✳✳✳✳✳

NO.645 - I've been out of it

Exp: when you are feeling tired and exhaust then you use this expression

Dialogue:

Where've you been?
I've been out of it for a few days.
The flu?
I don't know~ Just dead tired.

✳✳✳✳✳

NO.646 - to get my own way

Exp: She always gets her own way. Whatever she said to her mom, like if she wants to eat pizza, her mom accepts and give her pizza. If she want to go to the amusement park, Her dad or mom allow her to go to the amusement park. She gets everything what she want. So she always gets her own way.

Dialogue:

What do you want for dinner?
Hamburgers!
Not you! You always get your own way. Shane?
Um… I want…hamburgers!

✳✳✳✳✳

NO.647 – above/beyond reproach

Exp: if somebody is above reproach or beyond reproach that means, that person is perfect and he can't be criticized. You would never be disappointed in somebody.

Dialogue:

Did you hear about Bill Cosby?
It's disgusting~
I thought he was beyond reproach!
Are you kidding! No one in Hollywood is above reproach!

✳✳✳✳✳

NO.648 - tenacity

Meaning: determination, you don't give up,

Dialogue:

He's still there~
All day and nothing.

Not a bite. Just sunburn.
I respect his tenacity. Let's go!

NO.649 - to hang in the balance

Exp: if something is hanging in the balance, it means, you are waiting for result or decision; waiting for, it is good or bad.

Dialogue:

So, are you moving?
I don't know. It's hanging in the balance.
How's that?
If cats are okay, I'm moving. If not

NO.650 - auspicious

Meaning: favorable, auguring favorable circumstances and good luck

Dialogue:

Wow! You're all happy!
The boss' daughter is getting married.
So! Not to you!
But it's an auspicious day! I'm gonna ask for a raise!

NO.651 - smack-dab in the middle

Meaning: directly, precisely,

Dialogue:

Why are you covering your face?
I got a new zit.
Who cares!
It's smack-dab in the middle of my nose!

* * * * *

NO.652 - in the limelight

Exp: If some news/subject in the limelight means that everybody is talking about this new in these days. If a person is in the limelight that means that he is superstar, so everybody can see him.

Dialogue:

You're such a good singer!
Thanks^^
You should be a professional!
No, thank you! I hate the limelight

* * * * *

NO.653 - second to none

Meaning: the best,

Dialogue:

What's that?
Tangy Tangerine. Hmm^^
Is it any good?
Second to none! Wanna try?

* * * * *

NO.654 - peddling

Meaning: to sell something, sell or offer for sale from place to place

Dialogue:

Is that Coach Shane?
Yep. He's still peddling that DDM and PIRF stuff.
He should! They're second to none!
Really?
Everyone who joins stays and loves them!

✱✱✱✱✱

NO.656 - to KICK START smtg

Meaning: gat a lot of energy and power to get something moving, (we use it in business)

Dialogue:

Here you go, Shane!
Thanks, Santa! A new website?! WOW!
That's to kick start your business!
Oh, thank you SO much Santa!!

✱✱✱✱✱

NO.657 - to badger someone

Meaning: constantly ask the person question, usually same question,

Exp: do you like when some person badger you OR asking same thing. Every child badger with his parents.

Dialogue:

Let's go downtown and shop.
No. I hate the downtown area.
Why? It's exciting~ Come on~
No~ Everybody badgers you~ The bums, the sales people~

Please, please, please, please...
No! Now you're badgering me!

NO.658 - I can't thank you enough!

Exp: very good expression for saying thank you.

Dialogue:

Oh my god! This is so beautiful! I love it!
I knew you would love it—it's your style!
Yes! It's so beautiful! I can't thank you enough^^
Well, if you wear it every day, that will be enough thanks^^

NO.659 - whatever floats your boat

Meaning: whatever makes you happy

Exp: how many children you want to have. Somebody said 7 children. Oh my God, somebody want to have 7 children but whatever floats your boat OR have 7 children whatever makes you happy.

Dialogue:

Can you take me to the shopping mall?
Sure.
No, wait! Take me to Walmart instead.
Whatever floats your boat^^

NO.660 - saved the day

Exp: if your day is not going well, you are having problem, something bad was happing and somebody or something came and saved the day. Suddenly, because of that person or thing, everything became wonderful.

Dialogue:

David! I heard you got the job!
Yes, but it was Brittany. She saved the day~
What'd she do?
She woke me up in the morning! I would have been late

✳✳✳✳✳

NO.661 - to nosh (on something)

Meaning: to snack on something,

Dialogue:

You got anything to nosh?
Cheese.
Ooh, what kind?
Kraft Singles~

✳✳✳✳✳

NO.662 - a knee-slapper

Meaning: super funny,

Exp: my jokes are knee-slapper Or super funny.

Dialogue:

Did you hear Coach Shane's seagull joke?
No. Is it funny?
It is SUCH a knee-slapper! Check it out~
Okay, I will!

*****

NO.663 - PERIOD!

Meaning: I have nothing more to say,

Exp: I love writing books PERIOD! Usually, this expression use in negative meaning. I hate you PERIOD! And I am not going to say anymore.

Dialogue:

I saw some really nice shoes at the store~
I don't want shoes. I've got enough.
But they were on sale! And pink!
No shoes! Period!! ...Pink?

*****

NO.664 - I have a condition

Exp: My friend likes dark chocolate but he doesn't like dairy food like milk, curd, or milk chocolate. So one day, he went to the store and he looks some chocolate, so he asked him, "is that milk chocolate or dark?" person said "dark chocolate" So my friend bought and eat them. After 30 minutes later, another person told him "it was milk chocolate" So when he found the truth, he screamed "oh my God," and instantly, he runs to the bathroom. There was explosion. My friend has a condition OR medical problem/ allergic. So he should say to the person. "I have milk condition, so is this dark chocolate or milk chocolate."Then other person knows better him and know him that he has medical problem which might be horrible.

Dialogue:

Not too much salt. I've got a heart condition.
Okay.
Whoa, whoa! Slow down on the nuts.
Another condition?
Yep.
You're giving ME a condition~

✱✱✱✱✱

NO.665 - #to go

Meaning: remaining, left

Exp: I am trying to eat all cookies and I have 10 cookies and I start eating but then I full. My friends ask me "did you eat all cookies?" I say "NO, I have 2 to go" Or I still have 2 cookies reaming.

Dialogue:

Christmas is almost here!
Two days to go!
Will Santa be visiting?
I hope so! I was perfect ALL year!

✱✱✱✱✱

NO.666 - Your wish is my command^^

Meaning: absolutely, yes I will do it for you.

Exp: can you make me a sandwich? Can you take me a store?

 Yes, absolutely, your wish is my command.

Dialogue:

Coach Shane, can you do something special for us for Christmas?
How about a story about St. Nick?
Who's that?
That's another name for Santa Claus!
Yeah! That'd be perfect~
Your wish is my command^^

✱✱✱✱✱

NO.667 - a knuckle dragger

Meaning: act like a caveman or animal,

Dialogue:

Why don't you want to date Brian?
Brian? The knuckle dragger?
Come on! He's not that bad!
He's a CAVEMAN! PERIOD

*****

NO.668 - a living legend

Meaning: somebody who has done something amazing, (so every person respects him), true leader in one area,

Dialogue:

When I die, I want to be happy.
When I die, I want to be a living legend.
Uh, you need to be alive to be that.
Oh. Right. Yeah.

*****

NO.670 - to lose sleep over something

Meaning: I can't sleep because of

Exp: because of my bills, I can't sleep. I am thinking about bills. Because of my boss, I can't sleep. Or I am losing sleep over my boss. Because my boss is so mean. He makes me worry.

Dialogue:

You look really stressed.
Jack's having a New Year's Eve party. No invitation~

Eh~ That's nothing to lose sleep over. He's a jerk anyway.

Yeah...I guess. Did you get invited?

Yeah.

Argh~~~

＊＊＊＊＊

NO.671 - to draw a blank

Exp: if you are trying to remember your password or your friend birthday or your mother email or something else, but right now, you can't remember it. You know the answer but right now, nothing. So you can say "I am drawing a blank."

Dialogue:

What are you writing?

My resolutions, but I've drawn a blank.

You have nothing to improve?

I don't think so. I think I really am perfect.

＊＊＊＊＊

NO.672 - to break someone/to break a (bad) habit

Meaning: to stop the habit,

Dialogue:

You never smile.

I'm not used to showing my emotions.

I'll break you. I'll never stop trying to make you smile.

Good luck! I'm pretty tough~

＊＊＊＊＊

NO.673 - an invigorating sleep

Meaning: wonderful sleep, totally rested, very relax,

Exp: I have an invigorating sleep today, so I am very fresh right now.

Dialogue:

You look really good!
Yeah! Invigorating sleep is the key!
How do you get that?
Exercise, diet and meditation! Try it^^

NO.674 - to be filled with confidence

Dialogue:

I need a haircut.
You should go to my barber.
He does a horrible job on your hair.
Mine's curly—it's tough. It always grows back.
That's doesn't fill me with confidence.

NO.675 - full of himself

Meaning: love himself too much, he/she thinks that he is the greatest person and he never said or do something wrong.

Dialogue:

Are you throwing away this CD?
Yeah. No more U2 for me.
Why? The band's great!
But Bono's too full of himself! He should just stick to music.

*****

NO.676 - my soulmate

Meaning: unusually close to some person, your habit and likes are same with that person,

Dialogue:

mate/soul-mate are all possible!)
When are you gonna get married?
I'm still waiting for my soulmate.
Are you nuts? Nobody's like you.
There must be one person~

*****

NO.677 - to throw a temper tantrum

Exp: kids are temper tantrum. If they ask to you buy something and you don't do that, they would be crazy and will cry.

Dialogue:

Where's your daughter?
She's with the babysitter.
You didn't bring her to the store?
No way. She always throws a temper tantrum in the candy aisle!

*****

NO.678 - swing and a miss

Meaning: somebody tried to do something but unsuccessful,

Dialogue:

So, how was the restaurant?
Swing and a miss.
Really?
The staff, great. Service, good. Food, so-so. Cost, too much.

*****

NO.679 - telemarketers

Meaning: somebody who trying to sell something and talk to you in great detail,

Dialogue:

Hello? ... ~click~
Did you just hang up? No one there?
A telemarketer. I hate them.
Well, don't just hang up!

*****

NO.680 - STILL!

Meaning: anyway, (2) you have to,

Exp: a small boy gets small piece of cake on his birthday and he want more so he said to his mom "I need more cake", mom said "no, it's not good for your health", boy said "STILL!," OR "anyway, I need more cake".

Dialogue:

Telemarketers are such a pain.
Still, you should be polite.
But they're rude.
STILL! At least say goodbye!

*****

NO.682 - to iron out

Meaning: to solve problem

Dialogue:

Are you busy this afternoon?
No, why?
Let's iron out a few things, okay?
Okay... Um, do we have problems?
No. We have dress shirts

NO.683 - iffy

Exp: if you can't say yes OR no; you are not sure and it depend on time, money, whatever. You can say "situation is iffy."

Dialogue:

You coming over Friday?
It's iffy.
Why? Work?
No. Football. How big's your TV?

NO.684 - one step forward, two steps back

Meaning: doing worst (feeling)

Exp: you are learning something like English. Then after few months, you felt that English become more difficult and you are worst.

Dialogue:

How's your English going?
Ugh~ One step forward, two steps back.
^^ Where'd you learn that expression?
Coach Shane.
Well, it sounds like you're learning a lot!

NO.685 - when the rooster crows

Exp: I get up early in the morning when the rooster/cock crows.

Dialogue:

Wow! You're done exercising already?
Yeah! You ought to join me.
Well...what time do you get up?
When the rooster crows.

✳✳✳✳✳

NO.686 - label me -

Meaning: call me, think of me as, put me into category,

Dialogue:

Look at your flags! You must be a democrat.
Oh, don't label me, please.
A republican?
If you must label me, label me proud.

✳✳✳✳✳

NO.687 - raise your glass

Meaning: cheers,

Exp: there is very important news, congratulation, hope for the future, raise your glass.

"mom, raise your glass", mom up his glass and said "why" and then you said "I am starting writing books, yea"

Dialogue:

Do you want friends around the world?
Yes!
Do you want people to respect you and your culture?
Yes!
Then raise your glass to English! Communication is the answer!
I'll drink to that^

*****

NO.688 - roots

Meaning: come into existence, originate (2) the place where something begins, where it springs into being

Dialogue:

You like the area?
It's nice, but I don't wanna put my roots down here.
Why not?
It's too urban. I want my kids to grow up in the country.

*****

NO.689 - a bug zapper

Meaning: bug killer gadget,

Dialogue:

Online shopping again?
I'm looking at bug zappers!
Yay! No more skeeters!!
That's what I'm hoping for^

*****

NO.690 - flimsy

Meaning: very thin and insubstantial, week argument,

Dialogue:

A new desk?
Yeah, the last one was no good. Too flimsy.
Didn't you pay a lot for it?
No, it was cheap. This one is much better.

$$*****$$

NO.691 - hit me up

Meaning: ask me for something,

Exp: if you need something hit me up OR ask me. If you need some help in English, hit coach Shane up.

Dialogue:

If you want free English lessons, hit me up.
Really? What kinds of lessons?
Two—speaking and listening.
Great! I'll email you today^

$$*****$$

NO.692 - doesn't cut it

Meaning: don't meet standard, not good enough

Dialogue:

So, how are these curtains?
Nope. They don't cut it.
Why?
They're too thin and too short.

✳✳✳✳✳

NO.693 - scatterbrain

Exp: if your brain is everywhere and it is not concentrating, you won't be able to think well and doing job well. If somebody is scatterbrain, they are thinking about too many things; they have lots of stress, they are busy and they don't remember what to eat.

Dialogue:

Did you send out the lessons?
What lessons?
The free lessons you promised!
Oh~ I'm such a scatterbrain! I'll do it~

✳✳✳✳✳

NO.694 - tight

Meaning: close friend, best friend forever,

Dialogue:

Wow! I saw you talking to that guy.
Besher? Oh, yeah. We're tight.
But he's such a famous genius!
I know! And he's a really great kid^^

✳✳✳✳✳

NO.695 - a drag

Meaning: extremely boring,

Dialogue:

Are you okay?

Huh? Oh, yeah. I'm just studying English.

It looks like you're almost dead.

Ugh~ Grammar is SUCH a drag.

NO.696 - a bit of a handful

Meaning: wild, difficult to control,

Exp: last day, I was using software; it was a bit of handful OR difficult and complicated. Some kids are a bit of a handful.

Dialogue:

Can you take care of my Pugsy?

No!

Only for two days?

Pugsy's a bit of a handful! No!

NO.697 - doughboy

Meaning: fat guy,

Dialogue:

What's up, doughboy?

Hi! What'd you call me?

You heard me! Doughboy!

That's muscle!!!

NO.698 - a jock

Meaning: person who loves sports and exercise; and that person is physical healthy,

Dialogue:

You're all sweaty!
Yeah, just finished my ride.
And you were swimming this morning?
Yeah. I love working out.
Wow~ I didn't know you were a jock!

✳✳✳✳✳

NO.699 - is dogging me

Meaning: to follow, (2) bothering me

Exp: my brother is dogging me OR my brother is bothering me

Dialogue:

Did you work out today?
No. My hamstring is dogging me.
Oh, that's too bad.
Yeah. I'll take a few days of rest.

✳✳✳✳✳

NO.700 - my foot...my butt.my ss

Exp: "all 700 expressions were easy"...

"Easy, my foot..." what are you talking about; what do you mean, 700 expressions were easy, No way, it's not. Some of them were really difficult. "And that's the mean of this expression.

Dialogue:

Coach Shane is finished.
What?
700 expressions. All free. All on YouTube. Other teachers sell that stuff! But today was his last.

He's retiring.
Retiring my foot! He'll never retire!

THE END